for
beginners

AI for Image Recognition for Beginners

Build Systems That Can Identify and Classify Objects and Features in Images

AI for Image Recognition for Beginners

Printed in the United States of America

First Edition: 2025

This copyright page includes the necessary copyright notice, permissions request information, acknowledgments for the cover design, interior design, and editing, as well as the details of the first edition.

www.littlebiggiant.com

Introduction

A classroom went quiet. A screen showed a single photograph of a dog chasing a ball. A small box of code flashed words and then a bold line: dog. The students cheered. A poster on the wall read AI for Image Recognition for Beginners — Build Systems That Can Identify and Classify Objects and Features in Images. On the table lay a printed headline that mentioned a known fact: in 2012 a computer program cut error rates in a huge image-recognition contest in half, and that one change made machines suddenly much better at recognizing photos. The room smelled like markers and hot chocolate. One hand shook. "Is that real?" someone whispered. Another voice answered, "It names things faster than anyone can say them." A nervous laugh escaped. Eyes were bright, and a small knot of worry formed in the stomachs of a few students. Machines that could name pictures felt like magic. They also felt a little dangerous. The program got the dog right. It missed a skateboard once and called it a bench. That mistake sat in the back of every mind like a cold pebble.

Outside, rain smeared the window. The teacher tapped the screen and added a new picture. This time the photo was fuzzy, taken at dusk. The program hesitated, then suggested two options. Muffled confusion filled the room. "What if it sees the wrong thing?" a student asked, voice thin. The question hung there, honest and urgent. The class leaned forward. No long speeches came next. Instead, a simple promise: this book would explain how those flashes of code turn into careful decisions, how a machine learns edges, colors, and shapes, and how to teach it not to confuse a skateboard with a bench. Steps would be small. Explanations would be clear. The moment felt like standing at the edge of a lab where a new light flickers on for the first time. Everyone wanted to know what the next image would reveal. Could the next picture change everything they thought they knew about seeing?

Table of Contents

Chapter 1

Introduction to Image Recognition and Applications

You will be able to explain what image recognition is, name real-world uses, describe basic image data representations, and outline a high-level computer vision pipeline by the end of this chapter.

What image recognition is and real-world use cases

Image recognition is a way for computers to understand what is in a picture. It looks for patterns that help identify objects, scenes, textures, or actions. Think of it as teaching a computer to "see" and say what it sees, using examples it learned from. The basic idea is to take a picture, compare it to many learned patterns, and return a label or a set of labels that describe what's in the image.

In the real world, image recognition helps in many families of tasks. First, it helps organize photos. A photo app can tag pictures by what's in them—sunsets, dogs, cakes—so you can find images later just by searching for those words. Second, it helps people move around and stay safe. In cars that drive by themselves, cameras recognize traffic signs, other vehicles, and pedestrians to decide how to move. Third, in healthcare, image recognition assists doctors by pointing out potential problems in medical images, like identifying unusual shapes in X-rays or MRIs. Fourth, in factories and stores, cameras can spot defects on a line or check prices and shelf placement to keep things consistent. Fifth, it can improve accessibility, for example by describing a scene to someone who cannot see it or by helping screen readers with more accurate image captions.

Two small stories show how this works in practice. Case one: you upload a family photo to a cloud album. The system looks at the picture, notices a dog, and labels it "dog." Because of that label, the app can later offer a search like "dog photos" or group this image with other pet pictures. The recognition helps you find memories faster without typing long descriptions. Case two: you open a gardening app on your phone. You point the camera at a plant, and the app recognizes the species. It might tell you when it's ready to water, how much sun it needs, or if it's a plant that needs special care. In both cases, recognition doesn't just see pixels; it tries to understand what those pixels mean in the real world.

A helpful way to think about the shape of image recognition work is to compare it to learning from examples. You show a computer countless pictures labeled with what's in them. Over time, the computer notices patterns that often appear with the same label. When a new image comes in, the computer asks, "Which label best fits what I'm seeing?" The answer helps apps, cameras, and devices behave in smarter ways. This learning from examples is why image recognition has become so powerful across many fields. It also means that accuracy depends on the quality and diversity of the data the system has seen, plus how the underlying models are designed to learn from that data.

A few clarifications help prevent confusion. Image recognition can be used to identify broad categories (like “animal” or “car”), or it can be more precise (like “Labrador retriever” or “sedan with a roof rack”). It can also be used to locate objects in an image, not just name them. When the system points to where something is, that’s called detection or localization. These tasks share a goal—helping machines understand visual information—but they operate at slightly different levels of detail. The important takeaway is that recognition is not a single trick; it’s a family of methods that work together to interpret pictures in useful ways.

Real-world uses come with tradeoffs. Some applications need high accuracy and fast responses; others must handle a wide range of environments, like changes in lighting or occlusions where objects are partly hidden. As a result, designers choose data, models, and processing steps that fit the goal, the hardware, and the user's needs. The field is built on straightforward ideas—learn from many pictures, apply what you learned to new images, and measure how well you're doing. The hard part is getting enough representative data and making sure the system stays reliable when things change.

Types of image data and basic representations (pixels, channels)

An image is made up of tiny picture elements called pixels. Each pixel carries information about color or brightness, and when you put all the pixels together, they form the whole picture. The simplest kind is grayscale, where each pixel stores how light or dark that spot is. Grayscale images have one channel—the channel that carries brightness information. Color images use more channels; most common are three: red, green, and blue. Each pixel in a color image has three numbers, one for each color channel, and together they create the color you see.

Color depth describes how many possible values each color channel can have. A common depth is 8 bits per channel, which means each channel can take 256 different values. With three channels, that gives more than 16 million possible colors for a single pixel. In practice, higher color depth can help with subtle color differences, but 8-bit per channel color is the standard for many everyday images and apps.

Images come in different shapes and sizes. The height and width tell you how many pixels tall and wide the image is. A larger image can show more detail but needs more memory to store and more computing power to process. Some images are grayscale, with one channel; some are color, with three channels; some formats add an extra channel for transparency (alpha). When a computer reads an image for analysis, it also sees the arrangement of those channels across the image, not just the colors themselves. This arrangement—how channels line up with pixels and how pixels line up to form the whole image—matters for learning algorithms.

Beyond raw pixels and channels, images are often transformed into standardized representations before a model can learn from them. This can include resizing to a common size (so every image has the same number of pixels), normalizing the brightness values to a consistent scale, and sometimes converting colors from one space to another (for example, from a perceptual color space to a model-friendly space). These steps help a learning system compare images more reliably, even if the pictures came from different cameras or lighting.

Images also vary in how they're captured: photographs from cameras, frames from a video, or even synthetic images generated by computer graphics. Some images are clean and simple, used for teaching basic recognition. Others are noisy or cluttered, with many things in view at once. Understanding this variety is important because a good recognition system needs to handle both easy cases and tricky ones. To do well, a system benefits from seeing many examples that cover a range of lighting, angles, scales, and backgrounds.

In practice, you'll hear terms like resolution, channels, and color space. Resolution describes how many pixels fill the image; higher resolution means more detail but more data to process. Channels tell you how many color or intensity layers the image has. Color space is a way of organizing those colors, like RGB or grayscale, which helps with consistent interpretation. A practical takeaway is that the same scene can look quite different when viewed as a gray image versus a color image, or when captured at different resolutions, yet the underlying information about what's in the scene remains the same.

A second practical point: most image data you'll work with in beginner-friendly contexts is standardized for learning. This means images are often resized to a common size before feeding them into a model. It also means there's a standard range for the pixel values, typically 0 to 255 for 8-bit images, though many pipelines convert these values to a 0 to 1 range during processing. These conventions aren't magic tricks; they are conveniences that help learning systems finish their work reliably and predictably.

High-level computer vision pipeline and system components

At a high level, image recognition works by moving through a simple sequence of stages. You start with an image coming from a camera or file. Then you pass it through a preprocessing step. This step can include resizing to a standard size, normalizing brightness, and sometimes filtering to reduce noise. The goal is to put the image into a form that a model can understand consistently.

Next comes the model itself. This is the "brain" part of the system. The model looks at the processed image and produces outputs such as labels (what is in the image) or bounding boxes (where things are located in the image). In simple terms, the model tries to map patterns in the image to meanings. The outputs are not random guesses; they are statistical estimates based on what the model learned during training from many examples.

After the model, there is often a post-processing step. This step helps turn raw model outputs into useful information. For example, the system might pick the most likely label, combine results from multiple views, or smooth out inconsistent predictions over time in a video stream. The goal of post-processing is to present clear, useful results to the user or to the next part of a larger system.

Supporting components make this pipeline practical in real-world applications. Data storage and access are needed so pictures and labels can be saved, searched, and updated. Computing resources like CPUs or GPUs run the heavy calculations that learn from data and make predictions quickly. An interface layer connects the recognition system to apps, websites, or devices so you can see results and act on them. In larger systems, a monitoring component watches how well the recognition is performing over time, which helps engineers catch drift or bugs and keeps the system reliable.

Two simple scenarios illustrate the pipeline in action. Scenario A involves a photo-organizing app. The user uploads images, a preprocessing step standardizes sizes and brightness, a trained model assigns labels like “dog,” “beach,” or “mountain,” and a user-facing viewer presents the results with options to filter by label. Scenario B involves a smart camera in a store. The camera captures frames, preprocessing aligns them to the model’s expectations, the model detects items or anomalies, post-processing aggregates results across frames, and store staff can review flagged images to verify issues. In both cases, the same core steps are visible: capture, prepare, predict, and present.

A practical mindset for beginners is to remember three quick ideas. First, data quality matters as much as model design. If the images aren't representative of what you want to recognize, the system won't perform well in real use. Second, simpler ideas often work surprisingly well at first. Start with a straightforward preprocessing plan, a basic model, and clear outputs before adding complexity. Third, practical testing matters. Try the system in small, controlled situations before you scale up to more challenging environments. By keeping tasks small, you build a solid foundation you can extend later.

Key Takeaway: Image recognition lets computers see and describe what's in pictures by learning from many examples; the power comes from good data, clear goals, and a simple, reliable pipeline.

Coming up next: Subtittle: Preparing and Understanding Image Data. In Chapter 2, you'll learn how to collect datasets and organize data storage, how to annotate images with reliable labeling, and how to preprocess images with resizing, normalization, and careful train/validation splits. You'll see how these steps set up everything the recognition system needs to work well in real life.

Chapter 2

Preparing and Understanding Image Data

You will learn how to gather, organize, and prepare image data so you can train reliable image-recognition models.

1. Collecting datasets and organizing data storage

Start by deciding where your images will come from and how you will store them. Think of data as a library: every image should have a clear place and a clear label so you can find it again later. If you mix images from different sources, you may mix up what you're teaching your model to recognize. A simple, solid approach is to create a root folder called Dataset, then create subfolders for each class you intend to teach your model (for example: Dataset/cats, Dataset/dogs, Dataset/cars). Place every image into the folder that matches its class label. Keep a small, plain text file or a simple spreadsheet that lists each image file path and its class. This is your map for later steps.

Consistency is key. Use the same image format (like JPEG or PNG) and the same naming convention for files. A straightforward convention is class_name_timestamp.jpg, so you can tell what an image shows even without opening it. If you use images from multiple sources, note the source in a separate manifest so you remember where each image came from. This helps with accountability and future audits.

Think about data organization as early as possible. A clean structure saves time, prevents mistakes, and makes it easier to scale your project. If you grow from a few dozen images to thousands, you won't drown in a tangled mess. In practice, most teams create a small readme in the Dataset folder explaining the folder structure, naming rule, and any special considerations for specific images. A quick start looks like this: a folder per class, a simple CSV with columns for filename, class, and source, and a brief note about when the data was collected.

Example 1: You're building a beginner dataset with five classes: cats, dogs, cars, bikes, and trees. You place images in folders Dataset/cats, Dataset/dogs, Dataset/cars, Dataset/bikes, Dataset/trees. You keep a file, manifest.csv, with rows like image_path, class_label, source, and annotation_status. This makes it easy to see what you have and what needs labeling or checking.

Example 2: You pull a public dataset online and add it to Dataset, but you also take a small set of your own photos. You add a column in your manifest called provenance and another column for quality notes. You then run a quick visual spot-check on a random 5% sample to make sure images aren't corrupt and labels look reasonable. Small checks now beat big headaches later.

Hints that help you stay focused: label folders by class only; do not mix classes in a single folder. Keep a short glossary of class names to avoid typos (for example, "car" vs. "cars" vs. "automobile"). Maintain a simple backup plan so you can recover if something goes wrong. Finally, log any data-cleaning steps you perform, so you can reproduce them later.

Two quick micro-cases show the idea in action

Micro-case A: You receive a batch of 300 photos showing five classes. You sort them into five folders, check that each image clearly shows its label, and add a line in manifest.csv with the filename, class, and a brief note on lighting or blur if it's unusual. After this, you run a quick visual skim to confirm no mislabeled images sneaked in.

Micro-case B: You assemble a repository from two sources: a public dataset and your own photos. You copy the public images into Dataset/public and place your own photos into Dataset/own, then you merge an index file that records which source each image came from and whether you've annotated it yet. This keeps your future audits straightforward and honest.

2. Annotation methods and labeling quality control

Annotation is how you tell your model what's in the image. There are several ways to annotate, depending on what you want to teach your model to do. At a basic level, you'll provide labels—simple category names for what's in the image. If you want the model to locate things in the image, you'll add bounding boxes. For more precise work, you can use segmentation masks that outline the exact shape of objects. For beginners, start with class labels and, if you can, simple bounding boxes for a subset of images to learn how localization works.

Create clear annotation guidelines so anyone labeling the data uses the same rules. This reduces confusion and helps keep labels consistent. A practical guideline is to define each class with a short, concrete description and one or two example images. If you work with others, consider a quick cross-check where a second person reviews a sample of labels. This "inter-annotator check" helps catch mistakes early.

Quality control is a small investment with a big payoff. Build a simple review process: pick a random sample of 5–10% of your labeled images and check them for label accuracy and consistency. If disagreements appear, refine the guidelines and re-train the annotators. Keep a log of common mistakes and update the guidelines to prevent repeating them. If you can, maintain a basic version history of your annotations so you can revert if a labeling pass introduces problems.

Two micro-cases to illustrate labeling in practice

Micro-case A: You're labeling a set of 200 street-scene images with three classes: car, person, and bicycle. You prepare a short rule sheet: "Car means any vehicle with wheels; Person means a human figure; Bicycle means a two-wheeled rider." You assign one person to annotate and a second to validate. You review 10% of the results, find several mislabeled cars, and adjust the rule sheet. After updating, you re-run the sample check, and the rate of disagreement drops to near zero.

Micro-case B: For a small product-photos dataset, you annotate each image with a single label and a bounding box of the main object. You then run a quick inter-annotator check on 50 images labeled by two teammates. You find that one class name was used inconsistently (shirt vs. top). You unify the naming in the guidelines and re-label the few affected images. The labeling becomes cleaner and more reliable.

A practical labeling checklist

- Define each class with a short, precise description.

- Decide whether you'll use labels only, or labels plus bounding boxes, or segmentation masks.

- Create a short annotation guidelines document.

- Have at least one other person review a sample of labels.

- Keep a log of labeling decisions and changes to guidelines.

Periodically re-check a subset of labeled data to catch drift.

3. Preprocessing: resizing, normalization, and train/validation splits

Preprocessing turns raw images into a format a model can learn from. The goal is to present consistent input to the model and to separate data in ways that let you measure how well your model will perform on new images.

Resizing and aspect ratio

- Most models expect images at a standard size. Resize all images to a fixed width and height, such as 224 by 224 or 256 by 256. If an image doesn't match the aspect ratio, decide whether to crop or to pad with a neutral color so the content isn't distorted. In practice, preserving important objects is easier when you pad rather than crop aggressively.

- Keep a simple note of how you handled each image during preprocessing, so you can reproduce it later if needed.

Pixel value normalization

- Normalize pixel values so the model sees inputs with similar ranges. A common approach is to scale pixel values from 0–255 down to 0–1. Some workflows use zero-mean, unit-variance normalization, where you subtract a mean pixel value and divide by a standard deviation for each color channel. If you're following a standard backbone, use the normalization values recommended for that backbone to avoid mismatches.

Train/validation splits

- Split your dataset into training and validation sets so you can measure how well your model generalizes. A typical approach is to keep a majority of images for training and reserve a portion for validation. If you have a class with very few examples, try to maintain some proportion of those examples in both sets to avoid a biased evaluation. For beginners, a common starting point is an 80/20 split, adjusted to keep class distributions similar in both sets. If you're using a held-out test set later, you can allocate a separate portion for that as well.

Practical preprocessing steps you can implement this week

- Choose a target image size (for example, 224x224) and implement a resize-and-pad or resize-and-crop rule so every image ends up the same size.

- Apply a simple normalization to scale pixel values to 0–1, and optionally standardize color channels if you're using a backbone that expects it.

- Randomly shuffle your dataset and split it into training and validation sets, preserving class proportions.

- Save both the preprocessed images and a metadata file that maps preprocessed images back to their original sources and labels.

Two micro-cases that show preprocessing in action

Micro-case A: You have 1,000 images across five classes. You resize every image to 224x224, pad when needed to preserve aspect ratio, and normalize to 0–1. You then create a manifest.csv listing preprocessed_path, class_label, and split_label (train or val). The result is a neat, uniform dataset ready for the first training run.

Micro-case B: You notice a class with only 20 examples. You decide to apply an 80/20 split but ensure at least 4–5 instances of that class appear in the validation set so you can gauge performance on the rare category as you train. This keeps your evaluation honest as you start.

Exercises

1) Dataset architecture sprint (15 minutes). Design your Dataset folder structure on paper or in a quick document. Write down the naming rules for folders and a short manifest schema (columns you'll track). Measure progress by having a second person review your plan for clarity.

2) Annotation quality pilot (20 minutes). Annotate 10 images with labels (and, if possible, bounding boxes). Create a tiny guideline sheet and

perform a 5-image cross-check with a partner. Record any disagreements and revise the rules.

3) Preprocessing quick-start (25 minutes). Pick 50–100 images and apply a fixed resize-to-224 rule, pad where needed, and normalize to 0–1. Save a small sample set and create a short metadata file. Verify that all images load correctly in a viewer and show the expected dimensions and range.

4) Split sanity check (10 minutes). Randomize your data and divide into training and validation sets, keeping class distribution roughly the same. Compare class counts between train and val, and adjust if any class is underrepresented in either subset.

Troubleshooting quick fixes

- Images appear distorted after resizing: switch from aggressive cropping to padding to preserve content; verify aspect ratios and recheck the resize logic.

- Some images fail to load in your viewer after preprocessing: ensure file paths are correct and that no images were accidentally saved with the wrong extension.

- Class labels appear inconsistent across the dataset: update the labeling guidelines, run a quick cross-check with a partner, and unify naming (for example, all lowercase, no plural inconsistencies).

- Validation accuracy trends collapse early in training: revisit your split to ensure the validation set is representative; re-check that preprocessing does not introduce artifacts that systematically favor one class.

Templates and tools you can copy

- Dataset folder blueprint: Dataset/CLASS_NAME/ for each class; manifest.csv with columns filename, class_label, source, annotation_status, preprocessing_status.

- Annotation guidelines skeleton: a one-page doc with class descriptions, labeling rules, and examples.

- Preprocessing checklist: target size, padding/cropping rule, normalization method, train/val split ratio, and a note about maintaining metadata mapping original-to-preprocessed images.

- Quick verification script outline: a small script to confirm all images in manifest.csv exist in the dataset and have the expected dimensions after preprocessing.

Key Takeaway: Clear data structure and honest labeling make learning from images reliable and repeatable. Coming up next Subtittle: Fundamentals of Machine Learning for Images

1) Supervised learning, loss functions, and optimization goals,

2) Feature engineering versus end-to-end learning approaches,

3) Bias-variance tradeoff and techniques to avoid overfitting.

Chapter 3

Fundamentals of Machine Learning for Images

By the end of this chapter, you will know how supervised learning for images works, when to engineer features versus rely on end-to-end learning, and how to balance model complexity to avoid overfitting in practical projects.

Step 1: Understand the idea of supervised learning for images

You begin with a simple goal: teach a computer to recognize things in pictures by showing it many examples that are already labeled. Imagine you have a folder of photos, each one labeled with what it shows—a cat, a dog, a car, or a tree. You feed these labeled images into a learning system, and it tries to find patterns that connect the pixels on the page to the labels you gave. The computer learns from many such examples, refining its guesses over time so that when it sees a new photo, it can predict the label with reasonable accuracy. This learning process relies on mapping inputs (images) to outputs (labels) based on prior experience, not on hard-coded rules. It becomes powerful when the examples cover variations you expect in real life: different angles, lighting, backgrounds, and sizes. In practice, you test the system by giving it new images it hasn't seen before and watching how well it labels them. When the predictions are close to the true labels, you know the learner is capturing something real about the world. A micro-example can be a simple set of handwritten digits where each image shows a single number between 0 and 9. The learner's task is to identify which digit is drawn, based on the patterns in the pixels, not on any preexisting description of what a "3" or a "7" should look like.

Step 2: Dive into loss functions and the optimization goal

Loss functions are the guiding compass for learning. A loss function is a yardstick that tells the system how far its current guesses are from the truth. For image classification, a common choice is a loss that punishes wrong guesses and rewards correct ones in proportion to confidence. When predictions line up with the true labels, the loss is small; when they don't, the loss is large. The optimization goal is to minimize the average loss over many training examples. Think of it as a game where you adjust the internal settings of the learner so that, on average, it makes better and better guesses. The specific shape of the loss matters: a smooth loss helps you navigate toward better answers, while a very rough loss can mislead you or trap you in bad spots. In practice, you often pair a loss with a probability output: the model assigns a confidence to each possible label, and the loss punishes low confidence on the correct answer and high confidence on the wrong ones. A second micro-example shows how this works in a two-class problem, like distinguishing cats from dogs: the loss decreases as the model becomes more certain about its correct predictions, and increases when it confuses a cat for a dog.

Step 3: Understand optimization dynamics and practical training flow

Optimization is the method you use to reduce the loss over time. Most learners tweak their internal numbers—weights—by following the direction that lowers the loss the most. This is the essence of gradient descent and its smarter siblings.

You feed batches of images to the model, compute the current loss, estimate the direction to move the weights, and adjust a little bit at a time. The learning rate tells you how big each adjustment should be: too large, and you overshoot the best settings; too small, and progress becomes frustratingly slow. You can improve learning with ideas like momentum, which helps push past small bumps in the loss landscape, or learning rate schedules, which start with larger steps and gradually shrink as the model gets closer to a good solution. A practical illustration: you train your digit-recognizer for a few dozen passes over the data (epochs). Early in training, you see big jumps in accuracy as the model learns broad patterns; later, improvements come in smaller, steadier steps as the model fine-tunes what it already knows. The outcome you want is a model that performs well not only on the training set but also on fresh images it's never seen.

Step 4: Compare feature engineering with end-to-end learning

Feature engineering means you craft specific, hand-made descriptors that try to capture important aspects of images. Think about color histograms, edge detectors, texture summaries, or shapes you expect to matter for a given task. You feed these crafted features into a simpler learner, which then decides the labels. End-to-end learning, by contrast, lets the model learn its own internal features directly from raw pixel data. A deep neural network, for example, discovers helpful patterns without you telling it what to look for. The trade-off is clear: feature engineering can be effective when you have strong domain knowledge and limited data, and it often makes training faster because the input is already simplified. End-to-end learning shines when you have lots of data and compute, and you want the model to discover nuanced patterns that humans might miss. A micro-case to ground this idea: if you're trying to detect whether a photo contains a vehicle in a city scene, hand-crafted features like edge detectors might pick up straight lines and shapes typical of cars, but a neural network can learn to recognize complex cues like silhouettes, reflections, and context, all in one go.

Step 5: Grasp the bias-variance tradeoff and what it means for image tasks

The bias-variance tradeoff is a balancing act between two kinds of error. High bias means your model makes systematic mistakes, perhaps because it's too simple to capture the real patterns in the data. High variance means your model is too wobble-prone: it performs well on the training set but poorly on new images because it has learned noise rather than the underlying signal. For image problems, the danger often comes from making your model too complex for the amount of data you have, so it latches onto random quirks in the training images. You can spot this by checking performance on a separate validation set: if accuracy is high on training data but low on validation data, your model likely overfits. If both are low, underfitting is the issue. You don't have to chase perfection in either direction. Instead, you aim for a middle path where the model is just complex enough to capture the true patterns without memorizing the noise. A practical metaphor: you want a map that shows the major roads clearly without getting distracted by every tiny alley.

Step 6: Gather practical techniques to avoid overfitting and improve generalization

When your model is stickier than a post-it, you take steps to improve how well it generalizes. Start with regularization: add small penalties that discourage the model from relying on any single feature too heavily. For image models, this often means weight penalties that keep the internal connections from becoming too dominant. Data augmentation helps you pretend you have more data by slightly modifying existing images—rotating, flipping, cropping, or adjusting colors—so the model learns to recognize the same object in different looks. Cross-validation is another tool: you train on different subsets of your data and check consistency of performance to ensure you aren't overfitting to a single split. Early stopping is a simple, effective technique: you monitor how the model performs on a holdout set and stop training when accuracy stops improving, so you don't let the model memorize the training data. For more flexible models, you might adjust capacity: try a simpler architecture or fewer parameters if the data is limited, or add more layers and units if you have a lot of data. Finally, you can combine approaches: for some problems, feature engineering plus a modest end-to-end component can give you the best of both worlds. A two-scenario takeaway helps you practice: in a small dataset of animal pictures, prefer regularization and augmentation; in a large, varied dataset of street scenes, you can lean more on end-to-end learning with careful validation.

Examples and micro-cases to illuminate the steps

Example A: You're building a simple image classifier to tell whether a photo shows a dog or a cat. You start with a labeled set of thousands of dog and cat photos. You pick a cross-entropy loss and train a small neural network with mini-batches. You watch the training loss fall, but you also monitor the validation loss. After a while, the training accuracy continues to improve while validation accuracy stalls or declines. You suspect overfitting; you add a bit of weight decay (a small penalty on large weights) and apply horizontal flips to augment the data. Training resumes; validation accuracy improves again and stabilizes at a high level. The final model generalizes better to new dog-and-cat photos.

Example B: You're exploring feature engineering versus end-to-end learning for classifying plant species from leaf images. You first extract simple features: color histograms, edge counts, and texture descriptors. You train a straightforward classifier using those features and find reasonable accuracy with a modest amount of data. Then you try an end-to-end approach by feeding raw leaf images into a small convolutional network. With the same dataset, the end-to-end model learns to combine low-level cues into higher-level patterns and can outperform the handcrafted features, especially when leaves vary in lighting and background. The lesson: test both approaches on your data; choose the method that yields the best generalization, not the method you prefer in theory.

Exercises to practice the three points

1) Exercise: Identify a small image task and sketch two learning plans. Plan A uses feature

engineering with a simple classifier; Plan B uses end-to-end learning with a lightweight network. Time: 20 minutes. What would you expect to gain from each plan, and how would you measure success on a validation set?

2) Exercise: Pick a loss function for a two-class image problem (cat vs dog). Write down how the loss would penalize wrong predictions and how you would observe its decrease during training. Time: 15 minutes. Record a few training steps and note how quickly the loss drops.

3) Exercise: Design a quick mitigation for overfitting. Choose two techniques (for example, data augmentation and early stopping). Explain when you would apply them, how you would

monitor progress, and what signs would tell you to adjust.

4) Exercise: Create a tiny bias-variance diagnostic plan. List three signs of high bias and three signs of high variance you would look for during training and validation. Time: 10 minutes. Write a short plan for how you would respond if you saw each sign.

Troubleshooting quick fixes

Problem: The training loss drops fast but the validation loss stalls or rises.

Fix: Introduce some regularization, or reduce model capacity slightly, and increase data augmentation to help generalization.

Problem: The model never learns; both training and validation accuracy stay low.

Fix: Check data quality and labeling, ensure the data distribution matches what you expect, and consider starting with a simpler model or more robust features.

Problem: Gradients blow up or vanish during training.

Fix: Adjust the learning rate, use gradient clipping if available, and verify input normalization so the network starts in a stable regime.

Tools and templates you can reuse

1) Data readiness checklist: labeled images, clear categories, consistent labeling across the dataset, and a split into train and validation sets.

2) Loss and optimization plan template: pick loss, choose optimizer, set learning rate schedule, and decide when to stop.

3) Regularization and augmentation plan: list two to three regularizers and two augmentation techniques you will apply, with a rationale for each.

4) Bias-variance diagnostic sheet: a simple table to compare training and validation accuracy, plus notes on signs of underfitting or overfitting and proposed actions.

Key Takeaway: You balance data, model choice, and training tricks to build an image classifier that generalizes beyond your exact training set.

Coming up next

Convolutional Neural Networks Essentials

1) How convolutions, kernels, and pooling operate on images,

2) Common architectures (LeNet, AlexNet, ResNet) and their design ideas,

3) Layer types, receptive fields, stride, and padding explained

This is the path you'll take next, moving from the ideas behind learning from images to the building blocks that make image recognition possible at scale. You'll learn how to shave complexity with efficient architectures, how to think about the size and shape of each layer, and how receptive fields control what the network can see at different depths. As you practice, you'll begin to see how the concepts from this chapter become the practical decisions that drive real image systems. The next chapter will guide you through the core ideas of how those networks process images, so you can start experimenting with your own models and tasks, step by step.

Chapter 4

Convolutional Neural Networks Essentials

You will learn how CNNs read images, what makes LeNet, AlexNet, and ResNet work, and how the size and flow of information change as you choose different layer settings like stride and padding.

1) How convolutions, kernels, and pooling operate on images

Imagine an image as a grid of numbers, each number representing a tiny brightness or color piece. A convolution is like using a small stamp, called a kernel, to press over that grid. The kernel has its own tiny grid of numbers, and as you slide it across the image, you multiply the overlapping numbers and add them up. The result creates a new grid of numbers—the feature map—that highlights a pattern the kernel was looking for, such as edges or textures.

Key ideas you will use: a kernel is smaller than the whole image, and you move it across the image step by step. Each position gives you one number in the feature map. Do this with many different kernels, and you build many feature maps at once, each one telling you something different about the same image. This is how a CNN starts to "see" by learning which kernels pick out useful features.

Pooling is a sibling idea that helps the network see the bigger picture without getting tangled in tiny details. Instead of looking at every single pixel, pooling looks at small blocks and records a summary value, most often the largest value (max pooling) or the average value (average pooling). The effect is twofold: it reduces the size of the data, which makes processing faster, and it helps the network become a little tougher against small shifts or noise—things that can trick a precise pixel-by-pixel comparison.

Two micro-cases help you feel the mechanics without getting lost in math. Case A shows a tiny image, 4 by 4 pixels, and a 2 by 2 kernel moving with stride 1. As the kernel passes over each 2 by 2 block, you compute one number for every position. The resulting 3 by 3 map captures a simple pattern in the image. Case B moves into pooling: take a 4 by 4 region and apply 2 by 2 max pooling with stride 2. You end up with a 2 by 2 map that represents the strongest features in each 2 by 2 block. The network gains a compact view of the scene, preserving the most important signals while discarding tiny, exact details that aren't as helpful for recognizing objects.

When you combine several layers, the early convolutions might detect simple things like edges, corners, and textures. Deeper layers can combine those basic features into more complex patterns like shapes and parts of objects. The layout of kernels and pooling steps creates a pathway where information flows from raw pixels to higher-level understanding.

2) Common architectures (LeNet, AlexNet, ResNet) and their design ideas

LeNet. Think of LeNet as the classic starter kit for image recognition. It uses a few simple convolutional layers followed by pooling and then a couple of fully connected layers at the end. The design idea is to pull out local patterns early, then combine them into a decision about what the image shows. It's efficient and easy to study, which makes it a great teaching example for how a CNN builds from simple cues to a full answer.

AlexNet. This design kicked the door open for bigger, deeper networks. AlexNet uses more convolutional layers and larger feature maps, along with practical ideas that helped training at scale: rectified linear units (ReLUs) for faster learning, dropout to reduce overfitting, and a design that favors deeper feature extraction. The core idea is that by stacking more layers you can learn richer features, but you need strategies to train them well and keep the network from memorizing the data.

ResNet. The deep lesson here is the power of shortcuts. ResNet introduces residual connections that skip one or more layers and add the skipped input back into the later output. This helps gradients flow backward through many layers during training, so you can build very deep networks without the usual training problems. The design idea is "let the network learn the difference," not just more of the same layers. Residual connections keep training stable even as depth grows.

Two micro-cases help you see these ideas in action. Case 1 compares a simple three-layer pipeline (conv → pool → conv) with a deeper six-layer design that uses small, repeated blocks. The deeper version often learns finer, more reliable features because the network can keep improving without getting stuck. Case 2 looks at a situation where a deep network without residuals struggles to move information back to earlier layers. Adding skip connections makes it much easier for learning signals to reach the earliest parts of the network, so performance improves and training becomes smoother.

3) Layer types, receptive fields, stride, and padding explained

Layer types. A CNN is a chain of layers that transform data step by step. The main players you'll meet are input layers (the image itself), convolutional layers (the stamp-and-sum steps that create feature maps), activation layers (nonlinear helpers that make the network capable of learning complex patterns), pooling layers (downsampling to simplify and emphasize important signals), normalization layers (to keep learning stable), and fully connected layers (the classical "last mile" that makes a decision based on all the extracted features). You'll also see occasional dropout or other regularization tricks to keep the network from memorizing.

Receptive field. Picture each output element in a feature map as looking back at a patch of the original image. That patch is the receptive field. Early layers have small receptive fields, so they see only tiny parts of the image. As you stack layers, the receptive field grows, so deeper neurons are influenced by larger regions of the input. In practice, this means deeper layers can recognize bigger structures, like a whole eye or a mouth, rather than just a single pixel's edge.

Stride. Stride is how far the kernel moves with each step. A stride of 1 means you slide one pixel at a time, keeping the output size larger and more detailed. A stride of 2 or more skips positions, which reduces the size of the output quickly. Bigger strides speed up processing and cap complexity, but they also jettison some detail that might be useful for fine distinctions.

Padding. Padding adds a border around the input so the kernel can reach the edge of the image. If you pad with zeros, for example, a 3 by 3 kernel with stride 1 can keep the spatial size the same as the input. Padding gives you control over how the image shrinks as you stack layers, and it helps you preserve edge information that otherwise would vanish in deeper layers.

Two mini-examples clarify these ideas. Example A shows a 5 by 5 image going through a 3 by 3 convolution with stride 1 and padding 1. The output remains 5 by 5 in size, but every location in that output now carries a summary of a 3 by 3 region in the input. Example B shows how changing the stride to 2 shrinks the output to roughly half the width and height. This makes the network faster and less detailed, which can be helpful when you want quicker results or you're focusing on broader patterns rather than tiny textures.

Putting the three main points together, you can see how a CNN's job is to translate raw pixels into higher-level understandings, by sliding kernels that detect patterns, pooling to compress and emphasize key signals, and stacking layers that push from local details to global ideas. LeNet introduces the idea with simplicity, AlexNet broadens the approach for bigger tasks, and ResNet teaches you how to keep deep networks trainable by letting information flow through shortcuts. The way you arrange layers, set stride, and apply padding changes not just the answers you get, but how fast you get them and how much detail you keep along the way.

Key Takeaway: Convolutional neural networks turn small image patches into powerful pattern detectors by sliding tiny kernels, then compressing and stacking those detectors to see bigger structures; understanding how layers, stride, and padding shape the data helps you design networks that balance detail, speed, and depth.

Coming up next: Subtittle: Training Deep Models Effectively. You will learn about choosing optimizers, learning rate schedules, and warmup strategies; about batch size, epochs, and checkpointing; and about handling training instabilities like vanishing or exploding gradients.

Chapter 5

Training Deep Models Effectively

By the end of this chapter, you will be able to train deep image models more reliably by choosing the right optimizer, learning rate schedule, and strategies to keep training stable.

Step 1: Pick a solid optimizer and set a dependable baseline

You start with a simple, reliable baseline. The optimizer is the engine that moves your model's parameters in the right direction. Two common choices for image models are stochastic gradient descent with momentum and adaptive optimizers like Adam. SGD with momentum tends to be steady and can offer strong generalization when you tune its learning rate carefully. Adam adapts to each parameter's needs, which can help you get off the ground quickly, especially on diverse networks and datasets. As a baseline, pick one of these and run a short training to see how the loss trends over time.

Rationale: The optimizer shapes how quickly you learn and how smoothly you approach a good solution. A clear baseline helps you compare later changes to learning rate schedules and warmup.

Practical hint: Start with a moderate learning rate for your chosen optimizer and then observe the loss trajectory. If the loss drops quickly and then plateaus or wanders, you have early clues about whether the schedule or warmup needs adjustment.

Example 1 (small model, quick check): You train a compact CNN on a toy dataset with SGD and momentum. The loss falls steadily for a while, then settles into a gentle crawl. You note the time it takes to see diminishing returns and plan a schedule change.

Example 2 (larger model, quick start): You train a deeper network with Adam. The initial progress is brisk, and the network starts to generalize well after a few passes through the data. This sets a comfortable baseline to compare with future tweaks.

Step 2: Choose a learning rate schedule that matches your training

A learning rate schedule changes how aggressively your model learns as training progresses. Common options include constant learning rate, step decay, and cosine annealing. A constant rate is simple but can waste capacity as the model nears a good region. A step decay lowers the rate at specific milestones, which can help the model settle into a minimum. Cosine annealing smoothly reduces the rate toward the end of training, often helping final convergence without abrupt drops. Pick one that fits your dataset size and model depth, then compare how the training behaves under two different schedules if you can.

Rationale: A good schedule helps the training process explore broadly early on and settle more precisely later, improving both speed and final performance.

Guidance: If you're unsure, try a cosine-like schedule for deeper networks and a modest step decay for shallower ones. Monitor validation loss in addition to training loss to see how the schedule affects generalization.

Example 1 (cosine annealing, deeper network): You switch from a fixed learning rate to a cosine-like decay. Early in training, loss drops quickly; later, it flattens with small fluctuations. Validation accuracy climbs steadily and remains stable as the learning rate narrows.

Example 2 (step decay, lighter model): You use step-down drops at a couple of milestones. The model makes solid progress after each drop and continues improving, but you notice a moment of plateau just before the first drop. You decide to adjust the timing of the steps in the next run.

Step 3: Add warmup to smooth early training, especially for deep nets

Warmup means starting with a smaller learning rate and gradually increasing it to the target value during the first handful of training steps or epochs. This helps the model regions to settle in gently, avoiding abrupt parameter jumps that can destabilize training. Warmup is especially helpful when using adaptive optimizers or very deep networks, and it pairs well with complex schedules.

Rationale: Early instability can hurt the entire training run. A cautious start sets the stage for smoother optimization later.

How to apply: Define a short warmup phase at the beginning of training for your chosen optimizer and scheduling method. The exact duration can vary with data size and network depth, but the idea is to rise from a small rate to the full rate gradually.

Example 1 (warmup with Adam): You begin with a gentle warmup period before reaching the full Adam learning rate. The initial losses are more stable, and the model avoids sharp spikes that used to stall progress.

Example 2 (warmup with SGD): You apply a brief warmup to SGD with momentum. The early steps feel less jumpy, and the curve of training loss stays smoother as it descends.

Step 4: Align batch size, epochs, checkpointing, and early stopping with your goals

Batch size affects how accurately each step estimates the gradient and how much memory you need. Larger batches make training faster per epoch but can reduce the noise that helps generalization. Smaller batches give noisier updates but can improve generalization and work better on limited hardware. Pick a batch size that fits your hardware and feels stable during initial runs. Then decide how many epochs you'll run and how you'll checkpoint and possibly stop early.

Checkpointing is saving your model at intervals so you can resume if training stops or to compare states. Early stopping watches validation performance and stops training when improvement stalls. This saves time and helps you avoid overfitting.

Rationale: A thoughtful rhythm—batch size, number of epochs, and checkpoints—keeps training practical and reliable, while early stopping prevents wasted effort.

Two practical tips:

- Use a moderate batch size to keep training responsive on your hardware, and if you have more memory to spare, you can experiment with larger sizes on a few runs to compare generalization behavior.

- Schedule checkpointing at sensible intervals (not too frequent, not too sparse) and allow a final save near the end of training to capture your best model.

Example 1 (mid-size dataset, practical rhythm): You choose a comfortable batch size, run for a set number of epochs, and checkpoint every few thousand steps. If the validation loss stops improving for a while, you stop early and keep the best checkpoint.

Example 2 (very small dataset, cautious pacing): You use a small batch and a short training window with frequent checkpoints. You notice that rapid checkpoints help you spot when the model starts to overfit, so you adjust early stopping rules accordingly.

Step 5: Tackle training instabilities like vanishing or exploding gradients

Two classic problems appear in deep networks: gradients that vanish (become too small) and gradients that explode (become too large). Vanishing gradients slow learning in the earlier layers; exploding gradients can make training unstable and cause the loss to shoot up. You can address these with a few practical moves that don't require rethinking the whole model.

What to do:

- Normalize and stabilize: Use appropriate normalization layers and ensure weight initialization supports healthy gradient flow.

- Manage learning rate: If gradients explode, reduce the learning rate or adjust the schedule; if they vanish, consider a slightly larger learning rate or a different optimizer.

- Use gradient clipping: Cap the size of gradients so they don't shoot past a safe threshold. This keeps updates within a stable range.

- Consider residual connections or skip paths: When possible, design or maintain architectures that help gradient flow through the network.

- Keep an eye on architecture choices: Some designs naturally resist gradient problems; if instability persists, you may simplify the network or add regularization.

Rationale: Proactive checks and small fixes keep training alive and progressing, rather than letting instability derail your effort.

Two micro-cases to illustrate:

- In one run, exploding gradients appear as sudden spikes in loss. You apply gradient clipping and ease up the learning rate; the loss curve smooths, and training resumes progress.

- In another run, vanishing gradients slow the early layers. You switch to a normalization layer and verify that the initial weights are reasonable; the early layers begin to learn again and the overall training regains momentum.

Exercises

1) Optimizer exploration (15–30 minutes): Run two quick trainings on the same dataset and architecture—one with SGD (momentum) and one with Adam. Compare how quickly the training loss drops, how stable the curve is, and how the final validation metrics look. Record which felt more reliable and why.

2) Schedule a change (20–40 minutes): Take a single run and switch from a constant learning rate to a cosine-like schedule (or step decay if you prefer). Note how the loss behaves over time and whether the model finishes with a smoother or sharper end.

3) Warmup and clipping (20–40 minutes): Add a short warmup at the start and enable gradient

clipping during training. Observe whether early updates feel less jumpy and if the later steps stay within a stable range. Check if the validation curve becomes steadier.

4) Early stopping test (15–25 minutes): Set up an early stopping rule based on validation loss improvement. Run a training session and see how quickly training stops when improvements stall, and whether you end with a strong checkpoint among your saves.

Troubleshooting: quick fixes for common pitfalls

- If the training loss climbs or becomes unstable, try lowering the learning rate or shortening the warmup. Your model might be learning too aggressively early on.

- If the validation loss starts rising while training loss falls, the model is overfitting. Try earlier stopping, add regularization, or collect a bit more diverse data.

- If gradients look erratic or explode, enable gradient clipping and verify that the batch size aligns with your hardware capabilities. Check for numerical issues in data preprocessing.

- If the model stalls without progress, reassess the data pipeline: ensure data is clean, properly normalized, and fed to the network in a consistent order (or shuffled correctly). A broken data flow can mask as a training issue.

- If you notice slow progress across runs, test a different optimizer baseline and a lighter schedule to see whether the issue is optimizer-specific or related to data, architecture, or hardware constraints.

Templates and tools you can copy

- Training setup template:
  - Dataset: [path or name]
  - Model: [architecture]
  - Optimizer: [SGD/Momentum or Adam]
  - Learning rate: [value]
  - Schedule: [constant / step / cosine]

- Warmup: [on/off and duration]

- Batch size: [value]

- Epochs: [value]

- Checkpoint interval: [steps or epochs]

- Early stopping: [on/off, patience]

- Gradient clipping: [threshold on/off]

- Metrics to monitor: [training loss, validation loss, accuracy, etc.]

- Quick checklist:

- Baseline run completed

- Learning rate schedule chosen

- Warmup implemented (if used)

- Batch size and epochs decided

- Checkpointing configured

- Early stopping configured

- Gradient clipping enabled (if needed)

- Data pipeline verified

Key Takeaway: A reliable training routine comes from a thoughtful mix of optimizer choice, learning rate schedule, warmup, and disciplined monitoring; when you see instability, you adjust the knobs in small, testable steps.

Coming up next: Transfer Learning and Fine-Tuning

1) Leveraging pretrained models and selecting suitable backbones

2) Strategies for freezing, fine-tuning, and adapting weights

3) Techniques for low-data scenarios and domain adaptation

Chapter 6

Transfer Learning and Fine-Tuning

By the end of this chapter, you will be able to start with a pretrained image model, pick a backbone, and adapt it for your task even if you have only a small amount of labeled data.

1) Leveraging pretrained models and selecting suitable backbones

What a backbone does is simple in idea, even though the math behind it can be deep: it is the part of a neural network that learns to extract features from images. A pretrained backbone has already learned to see edges, textures, shapes, and patterns from a huge set of images. You can reuse those learned features and adapt them to your own task, which saves you time and often improves accuracy compared to starting from scratch.

Start by thinking about what you're trying to recognize and how big your images are. If you have a relatively small dataset or you're running on a modest computer or a phone, you might choose a lighter backbone. A lighter backbone tends to be faster and eats less memory, which can be a big win in practice. If you're aiming for higher accuracy and you have more computing power, a deeper backbone that's proven effective on many tasks can give you stronger features to work with. The key is to match the backbone to your data and your hardware, not just to chase the latest model.

Next, check compatibility with your dataset. The final step classifier must match the number of categories you want to identify. If your project has ten classes, you'll replace the final layer so it outputs ten scores. If your input images are color images with three channels, keep that expectation the model will see when you feed it data. If your data look quite different from the images the backbone was trained on, plan on some extra adaptation later, but don't be discouraged—the backbone still gives you a strong starting point.

A practical approach is to start with feature extraction. In this mode, you freeze the backbone's weights and train only a new classifier head on top. This lets you see how well the learned features separate your classes with minimal risk of overfitting. When you feel ready, you can unlock more layers and fine-tune a small portion of the backbone. The idea is to move from relying on general features to letting the model tailor those features toward your specific task. Think of it as gradually teaching the model to see your problem the way you do, without throwing it into the deep end all at once.

Here are two micro-cases to illustrate the idea. Case A: You have a dataset of bird photos, with varying backgrounds and lighting. You choose a well-known backbone pretrained on ImageNet, replace the final layer for your 20 bird species, and start with the backbone frozen. You train only the last layer and the new classifier head. You'll often see a clean improvement because the backbone already knows how to detect edges and shapes birds use. Case B: You're building a projector-camera app that classifies plant leaves, where the images come from different cameras and the leaves look a bit different from standard photos. You pick a backbone that has shown good generalization, keep the backbone mostly frozen, and plan a later step to gradually fine-tune a small portion of the network. This helps the model adapt to the new domain without losing the broad image understanding it already learned.

The backbone choice also shapes what you can do next. If you see that your data can benefit from more specialized features—textures, fine-grained shapes, or color patterns—prepare to selectively fine-tune higher layers or a few blocks of the backbone. If you want a fast prototype or you're constrained by hardware, a smaller backbone with a lightweight classifier may be the best choice to get something working quickly and then improve it later.

2) Strategies for freezing, fine-tuning, and adapting weights

Now you'll move from "start here" to "start carefully." The core idea is to preserve what the pretrained model learned while allowing enough flexibility to adjust to your data.

Step 1: Decide your primary approach. For a small dataset or a quick prototype, begin with feature extraction: keep the backbone fixed and train only the new classifier. This gives you a solid baseline with minimal risk of overfitting. If you have a bit more data or you want higher accuracy, you'll gradually move toward fine-tuning.

Step 2: Freeze layers in blocks. You can freeze most of the backbone and train only the last few layers and the new classifier. When you're ready, unfreeze a few blocks at a time and train again. This staged unfreezing helps you find a balance between keeping helpful generic features and letting the model specialize to your task.

Step 3: Unfreeze gradually. Move from freezing most layers to only freezing the earliest layers, which tend to learn the most general features like edges and simple textures. Unfreezing in stages gives you more control and can prevent sudden, large changes that destabilize learning.

Step 4: Use different learning rates for different parts. The new classifier and any newly added layers usually benefit from a larger learning rate, while the pre-trained backbone often needs a smaller one. A common pattern is to keep a smaller learning rate for the backbone and a larger one for the classifier. This helps avoid destroying the useful features the backbone already has learned while still letting the model adapt quickly where it matters.

Step 5: Regularize to avoid overfitting. When you begin to fine-tune, your model has more capacity to memorize your data. Use proper regularization techniques—dropout, weight decay, and careful normalization—to keep the model generalizing to unseen images. Regularization helps you keep the benefits of pretraining while avoiding the pitfall of training too hard on a small dataset.

Step 6: Monitor progress with careful validation. Watch the gap between training and validation performance. If the gap grows, you may be overfitting and need to back off on fine-tuning or add more regularization. If validation performance improves with unfreezing certain layers, keep going in that direction, but never lose track of your validation results.

Two micro-cases to see these strategies in action. Case 1: You have 1,000 labeled plant images, and you start with the backbone frozen and the new classifier trained. After a few epochs, you test on a held-out set and notice modest gains but a slight overfitting signal. You then unfreeze the last two blocks of the backbone, keep the learning rate for the backbone low, and train again. The validation accuracy improves, with a stable gap between train and validation. Case 2: A small video-frame dataset for motion classification uses a backbone pretrained on a similar task but with different lighting. You begin with feature extraction, then gently unfreeze the top layer and adjust the learning rates. The model begins to capture the new lighting cues without losing the general edge-and-shape features it already had.

A crucial point here is to keep things practical. You don't need to become a tuning wizard overnight. Start with a clear plan: begin with a safe baseline (feature extraction), measure progress, then gradually allow more parts of the model to learn from your data. If you see instability, back off—lower the learning rate, reduce the unfreezing scope, or reintroduce more regularization. The goal is steady, incremental improvement, not a dramatic, risky change.

3) Techniques for low-data scenarios and domain adaptation

When data are scarce, your strategy shifts toward making the most of what you have, plus smart ways to bridge the gap between sources and targets.

Step 1: Amplify data through augmentation. Augmentations simulate new views of your images: slight rotations, flips, color jitter, crop transformations, and other benign alterations. These techniques teach the model to look for the same object even when its appearance changes due to angle, lighting, or partial occlusion. The key is to increase diversity without creating unrealistic examples. Well-chosen augmentations can dramatically improve generalization in small datasets.

Step 2: Bring in synthetic data carefully. If you can generate synthetic images that resemble your real task, you can expand your training set. The idea is not to overwhelm the network with fake data but to fill gaps that real data cannot cover—different backgrounds, lighting conditions, or rare viewpoints. Use synthetic data as a supplement, not as a replacement for real images.

Step 3: Tackle domain differences with simple alignment tricks. When your training data come from a different domain than your deployment data (for example, photos taken in one country vs. another, or studio images vs. field images), consider approaches that reduce the mismatch. That could be through normalization choices, matching color statistics, or training the final classifier on features that are robust to these differences. The goal is to reduce the domain shift so the learned features stay useful in the new setting.

Step 4: Targeted fine-tuning for small domains. If you have a handful of labeled examples from the target domain, you can fine-tune the upper layers with a small learning rate and strong regularization. This lets the model adjust to nuances of the target domain without losing the broad, transferable knowledge it gained during pretraining.

Step 5: Few-shot and prototype thinking. In some cases, you can use few-shot ideas where you form class prototypes from limited examples and measure similarity to new images. While you don't need a full few-shot algorithm, keeping the mindset of "how does this image relate to that prototype" can guide your design choices and help you reason about which features matter most.

Two micro-cases for low-data and domain adaptation. Case 1: You're classifying rare mushroom species with only 50 labeled pictures per species. You start with a strong backbone, train a classifier head, and apply aggressive augmentation to cover many appearances. When you see overfitting, you freeze more layers and choose a smaller learning rate for the backbone while keeping a bit more aggressive for the classifier. The result is steady improvement in validation accuracy as you expose the model to more variations without overwhelming it. Case 2: You want to deploy a fruit detector in a different country where fruit varieties look a bit different due to season and lighting. You train on your original dataset and then perform a light fine-tuning with a small set of local images, keeping most of the backbone fixed. The model adapts while preserving general knowledge about fruit shapes and colors.

Troubleshooting common obstacles you may encounter. If your model memorizes the training set and fails on new images, increase augmentation, add regularization, or simplify the model. If the backbone's features don't seem helpful for your task, try unfreezing a few higher layers and train with a smaller learning rate, or consider a different backbone that balances general features with task-relevant ones. If you see a big gap between training and validation performance after fine-tuning, slow down the unfreezing process, reintroduce stronger regularization, or re-check your data labeling quality. When domain shift causes a drop in accuracy, lean on augmentation that simulates the target domain, and consider a light domain-adaptation step to align features across domains.

Key Takeaway: Start with a pretrained backbone, move from fixed features to careful, gradual fine-tuning, and use data and domain adaptation strategies to stretch what little data can do for you.

Coming up next: Augmentation, Regularization, and Data Strategies

1) Image augmentation methods and how they improve generalization

2) Regularization tools: dropout, weight decay, and batch normalization

3) Using synthetic data, cropping, and domain randomization approaches

Chapter 7

Augmentation, Regularization, and Data Strategies

You will learn practical augmentation, regularization, and data strategies that boost image recognition models' ability to generalize, even when you have limited real data.

Augmentation for Generalization

1) Start with a clear baseline. You should know what your model already sees in training data and how it performs on a separate validation set. The goal of augmentation is to expose the model to a wider variety of appearances, so it learns to focus on the essential signals rather than incidental details. Think of augmentation as a way to pretend you have many more pictures than you actually do.

2) Choose transformations that reflect real variation. Use a mix of geometric and color-based changes. Geometric changes include horizontal flips, small rotations, translations, and slight scaling. Color-based changes include brightness, contrast, saturation, and color jitter. Add a touch of blur or noise to simulate different camera qualities.

Use these transforms sparingly and in combination; the idea is to broaden the training distribution without corrupting the labels or destroying recognizable features.

3) Apply transformations with thoughtful probability and magnitude. Don't flip every image or rotate every time. Instead, apply each transformation with a moderate probability (for example, 0.3 to 0.5 for many augmentations) and keep magnitudes small to moderate. If a transformation makes a picture look unrealistic, dial it back. The right balance prevents the model from learning to rely on a single cue that only appears in your original dataset.

4) Build a simple augmentation pipeline and test its impact. Create a pipeline that randomly applies a subset of transforms to each image. Run experiments where you compare the baseline model to versions trained with augmentation. Look for improvements in validation accuracy and more stable loss curves. If you see a drop, adjust magnitudes or remove the most disruptive transforms.

5) Use targeted augmentations for specific challenges. If your data comes from varied lighting, emphasize color and brightness changes. If objects appear at different angles, emphasize small rotations and crops. If you have occlusions, try cutout-like techniques that randomly mask parts of

images. The goal is not to confuse the model with chaos, but to teach it to recognize objects even when details shift.

6) Include a couple of concrete micro-cases. Micro-case A: You have a small dataset of everyday objects with about 1,000 images per class. Adding horizontal flips and small color jitters doubles visible variation without changing the core appearance, and validation accuracy increases by a noticeable margin. Micro-case B: A set of product photos taken under different lighting—sunlight, shade, and indoor lamps. Using random cropping and mild brightness adjustments helps the model identify the same product across lighting

conditions, reducing misclassifications when lighting changes.

7) Keep an eye on data quality during augmentation. If your augmentation produces images that look off or labels become unreliable (for example, rotating a sign so text becomes unreadable), stop applying that transform. Quality stays essential; augmentation should extend capability without muddying the signal.

Regularization Tools

1) Understand why regularization helps. Regularization encourages the model to find simpler, more robust patterns rather than

memorizing training examples. It reduces overfitting, which happens when a model performs well on training data but poorly on new data. Regularization works best when paired with a reasonable model size and good data processes.

2) Add dropout where it makes sense. Dropout randomly removes some units during training, forcing the model to rely on multiple pathways to make a prediction. In many networks, dropout is most effective in fully connected layers or after high-capacity blocks where overfitting tends to appear. Start with modest dropout rates (for example, 0.2 to 0.5 in the relevant layers) and adjust based on validation performance. If you use batch

normalization, be mindful that extreme dropout can reduce its stabilizing effect.

3) Use weight decay (L2 regularization) to constrain weights. Weight decay discourages the model from growing very large weights, which can lead to unstable learning and overfitting. Turn on a gentle L2 penalty on the weights and tune the strength based on how quickly the validation gap closes. The idea is to keep the model's parameters from chasing noise in the training data.

4) Integrate batch normalization to stabilize learning. Batch normalization helps by normalizing the inputs to each layer, which makes training less

sensitive to weight scale and learning rate. It can indirectly reduce the need for very high learning rates and can improve generalization. When you introduce batch normalization, monitor how it interacts with dropout and weight decay, because the combination can affect learning dynamics.

5) Pair regularization tools thoughtfully. A common approach is to combine modest dropout with weight decay plus batch normalization. Don't stack too many strong regularizers at once without monitoring, because they can dampen learning too much or make optimization behave oddly. Start with one change, measure its impact, and layer in the others gradually.

6) Ground your choices in small experiments. For a compact CNN trained on a modest dataset, adding dropout and weight decay often yields clearer gains than changing the architecture alone. If you see a flatter training curve but little validation improvement, reconsider the regularization strengths or try adjusting the learning rate schedule to let the model train more effectively with regularization.

7) Micro-cases to illustrate the idea. Micro-case A: A mid-sized CNN trained on a dataset with 5,000 images per class benefits from modest dropout in the final layers and a small weight decay, yielding steadier validation accuracy across epochs. Micro-case B: A deeper network trained with batch

normalization sequences shows faster convergence and less sensitivity to the initial learning rate, with better generalization on held-out data.

Data Strategies

1) Use synthetic data to cover gaps your real data doesn't reach. When certain scenes, angles, or textures are rare in your real dataset, synthetic data can fill the void. The principle is simple: if the real data misses a type of variation, can a plausible, labeled alternative help the model learn to recognize the same concepts under new conditions? If the answer is yes, synthetic data can be a practical stand-in.

2) Exploit cropping and patch-based views. Cropping creates smaller, sometimes harder-to-see views of objects. This forces the model to identify core features that persist across partial visibility. When used wisely, cropping improves robustness to object size and partial occlusion without sacrificing too much signal.

3) Embrace domain randomization to bridge gaps between synthetic and real data. Domain randomization deliberately varies textures, backgrounds, lighting, and even camera noise during synthetic data generation. The idea is to push the model to focus on the essential structure of objects, not the exact look of the scene. If real-world data is scarce or diverse, domain

randomization can help the model transfer what it learned from synthetic examples to real-world images.

4) Build a pragmatic data mix. Combine real data with synthetic samples to balance representation across classes and conditions. You don't need equal numbers of real and synthetic images; you aim for a distribution that reduces blind spots in real world variation while preserving label fidelity and realism where it matters most.

5) Be deliberate about data quality in synthetic sources. Even though synthetic data can be abundant, it should be labeled accurately and

reflect the concepts you want the model to learn. If synthetic data introduces unrealistic artifacts, it can mislead training. Start with simple, well-formed synthetic examples and increase complexity gradually as the model's understanding grows.

6) Micro-cases that show the idea in action.
Micro-case A: You have a collection of real product photos with uneven lighting. You generate synthetic variants with controlled lighting and background variations and blend them with real images. The model's ability to recognize products under unusual lighting improves noticeably.
Micro-case B: You're training a model to recognize household objects from multiple angles. Synthetic renderings of those objects from varied viewpoints,

paired with real photos, help the model generalize to new angles found in daily life.

7) Keep track of data provenance and labeling. Document where each image comes from, how it was created, and any transformations applied. Clear records help you adjust strategies if the model's performance wobbles and you need to trace which data sources contributed most to improvement or confusion.

Key Takeaway: Augmentation, regularization, and data strategies work together like a toolkit: augmentation broadens what the model sees, regularization keeps learning stable, and smart data strategies fill gaps that real data alone can't cover. Used together, they help your model recognize objects reliably across a wider range of conditions.

Coming up next Subtittle: Evaluation, Metrics, and Model Debugging

1) Choosing metrics: accuracy, precision, recall, F1, and mAP,

2) Managing class imbalance, threshold tuning, and cross-validation,

3) Visualization and error analysis to uncover model failure modes

Chapter 8

Evaluation, Metrics, and Model Debugging

You will learn how to pick the right metrics, handle imbalanced data, and spot why your model makes mistakes, so your image-recognition system becomes more reliable in real life.

Choosing metrics: accuracy, precision, recall, F1, and mAP

1) Start by identifying the core goal of your task. If you mainly care about overall correctness on a balanced dataset, accuracy is a straightforward starting point. If some mistakes matter more than others (for example, missing a rare but important object), you'll want to look beyond accuracy. Relying on one metric can hide problems, so pick a primary metric and use others to check the full story.

Rationale: Different tasks reward different signals, and a single number rarely tells the whole truth.

2) Learn what each metric measures in plain terms. Accuracy = how often you're correct overall. Precision = when you say something is a certain class, how often you're right. Recall = when that class is present, how often you find it. F1 = the balance between precision and recall, especially helpful when you need a middle ground. For object detection or segmentation, mAP (mean Average Precision) summarizes how well you rank true positives across thresholds.

Rationale: Knowing what each number actually reflects helps you interpret results without guessing.

3) Use a simple example to see the difference. Suppose your model labels images as "cat" or "not

cat." If you miss many cats but rarely mislabel non-cats as cats, recall might be low while precision stays high. If you label many images as cats and only a few are, precision will drop even if accuracy looks decent.

Rationale: Concrete situations show why the metrics disagree and when to look deeper.

4) Decide when to favor a metric other than accuracy. In a wildlife detector, you might prefer high recall so you don't miss rare animals, even if precision drops a bit. In a safety-critical system, you might prioritize high precision to avoid false alarms. Choose thresholds that align with this preference.

Rationale: Metrics are tools; pick the ones that match your real-world trade-offs.

5) Create a simple, repeatable reporting checklist. Record the primary metric first, then report at least two supporting metrics (for example, accuracy and F1, plus mAP if you're doing detection). Include a short note on the threshold used for decision making.

Rationale: Consistency makes it easier to compare models over time and across experiments.

Two micro-cases to show the steps in action

- Case 1: Balanced cats-versus-dogs. You measure accuracy as your main metric and confirm precision and recall are both high across classes. The model's confusion matrix shows a healthy balance between mislabeling cats as dogs and dogs as cats, reinforcing that you're not biased toward one class.

- Case 2: Rare-object detector. Your dataset has many non-target images and only a few with the object of interest. Accuracy stays high even when the model misses rare targets. If you only watch accuracy, you'll miss a crucial flaw. Precision, recall, and especially mAP reveal that the detector misses many true positives, guiding you to collect more examples of the rare class or adjust thresholds.

Tools you can use or copy: a small metrics sheet that lists tasks, primary metric, secondary metrics, thresholds used, and a quick interpretation note. Keep it near your training logs.

Managing class imbalance, threshold tuning, and cross-validation

1) Detect imbalance by checking how many examples each class has. When some classes are far more common, the model can become biased toward predicting those classes, which hurts performance on the rare ones.

Rationale: The data's shape often drives the model's behavior more than any single tweak.

2) Choose balancing strategies that fit your data. You can augment the minority class with more images, undersample the majority class, or use cost-sensitive learning that treats misclassifying rare objects as more costly. Data augmentation can help the model see more variations of the rare class without needing new real images.

Rationale: Balancing helps the model learn useful patterns for all classes, not just the majority.

3) Use threshold tuning to control precision and recall. For a classification task, you can adjust the decision threshold for the positive class to trade off false positives for false negatives. If you want to

catch more rare objects, lower the threshold to increase recall; if you want to reduce false alarms, raise it to increase precision.

Rationale: Thresholds give you a practical lever to meet real-world requirements without retraining.

4) Apply cross-validation to estimate how your model will perform on new data. With k-fold cross-validation, you train on different splits and check how stable your metrics are across runs. It's a guard against overfitting to one particular split of data.

Rationale: A robust estimate helps you avoid chasing a lucky result from a single train-test split.

5) Build a simple decision flow for when to rebalance, tune thresholds, or re-split data. If performance on rare classes is below a chosen level across folds, try targeted augmentation or collecting new samples. If precision and recall trade-offs don't meet your criteria after threshold tuning, consider adjusting the class weights or the model's architecture.

Rationale: A plan reduces guesswork and speeds up iteration.

Two micro-cases to show the steps in action

- Example 1: Medical-imaging class imbalance. Your dataset has far fewer positive cases than negatives. You use oversampling of the positive class and a higher weight for misclassifying positives during training. After rebalancing, recall improves, while you monitor precision to ensure it doesn't drop too much.

- Example 2: Wildlife detection with rare elk. You start with a modest threshold, measure recall, and find you miss elk too often. You then lower the threshold and add a small amount of targeted data around elk features. The elk detections rise, and you recheck precision to ensure the system remains usable in the field.

Exercises

1) For 10 minutes, list the three most important metrics for your task and explain why each matters. Record at least one concrete example from your data where each metric would tell you something useful.

2) Take two model runs with the same architecture but different class weighting. Spend 15 minutes comparing accuracy, precision, recall, and F1. Note how the weight changes affect each metric.

3) Create a small cross-validation plan (5 folds). For each fold, write down which metrics you'll report and how you'll summarize them. Do this in 20 minutes, then summarize the overall result in a short paragraph.

4) Pick one rare class in your dataset. For 15 minutes, design a minimal augmentation plan

focused on that class. After you train, check whether recall for that class improved and whether precision for it stayed acceptable. Record the before-and-after numbers in a tiny log.

Troubleshooting

- If accuracy looks good but recall is poor on a minority class, try targeted augmentation or a small change to class weights to boost learning on that class.

- If mAP is low despite high accuracy, recheck the detection thresholds across different recall levels and inspect a few misdetections to see if size, occlusion, or blur are the root causes.

- If threshold tuning swings precision and recall in opposite directions too aggressively, consider using a calibrated threshold per class or a simple ensemble decision rule that combines multiple metrics.

- If cross-validation shows large variance between folds, inspect data splits for leakage or correlated samples; you may need more diverse training data or stratified folds to keep class proportions balanced.

Templates and quick-checklists you can copy

- Metrics Quick-Check

Primary metric: ________

Supporting metrics: ________, ________

Threshold used: ________

Notes on interpretation:

____

- Cross-Validation Plan

Folds: _____

Metrics to report per fold: ________

How to summarize: ________

Decision rule after results: __________________

- Threshold Tuning Guide

Target objective: ________

Range to test: ________

Steps to evaluate: ________

When to finalize threshold: _____________

Coming up next

Subtittle: Deployment, Inference, and Scaling

1) Exporting models, quantization, and inference acceleration techniques,

2) Edge vs cloud deployment considerations and hardware choices,

3) Monitoring performance in production, versioning, and rollbacks

Chapter 9

Deployment, Inference, and Scaling

You will be able to export models, deploy them on edge or cloud, and monitor performance in production with a plan for versioning and rollback.

Exporting models, quantization, and inference acceleration techniques

1) Start with a run-ready format that fits your target environment. Think of your model's final form as a delivery package. For many projects, you'll choose formats that balance portability with ease of use on your chosen hardware. TorchScript works well for PyTorch-based projects, because you can freeze the model and run it in a Python-free environment. ONNX provides cross-framework compatibility, which helps if you want to swap frameworks later or run on different runtimes. CoreML can be the right fit if you're delivering to Apple devices, because it's optimized for iOS hardware. Pick the one that aligns with where your users will run the model most often, and where your tooling is strongest. The general rule: aim for a format that minimizes surprises during deployment

and lets you validate performance without re-implementing parts of the model.

2) Make the model lighter without destroying usefulness. Quantization is a common, practical path here. It reduces precision from full floating-point to lower-bit representations, which decreases memory usage and speeds up arithmetic on many devices. You can start with post-training quantization to see how much you gain and where accuracy might shift. If you know you'll run on devices with limited compute, consider quantization-aware training so the model learns to cope with lower precision during its actual training iterations. Pruning and distillation are other tools in the toolbox, used when you need smaller

footprints or faster inference without a heavy hit to accuracy. The guiding principle is simple: any size or speed gain should be verified against the actual tasks your users care about, so you know you aren't trading critical accuracy for speed.

3) Accelerate inference, but test carefully. After you choose a format and apply quantization or pruning, test the model on the hardware where it will run. Look at latency under typical load, not just peak speed in a quiet lab. Some runtimes offer acceleration back-ends that take advantage of specialized hardware. For example, you may see faster results on GPUs with optimized libraries, or on edge devices with CPU-friendly runtimes. The key is to compare apples to apples: measure the

same input sizes, preprocessing steps, and batch behavior you expect in production. If acceleration introduces small accuracy changes, document them and decide whether they're acceptable for your use case. If not, you may need to revisit the quantization strategy or adjust the model slightly.

4) Package with environment and compatibility details. A robust deployment needs clear packaging: which runtime, which version of libraries, and which hardware assumptions it requires. Include a minimal tutorial for engineers who will integrate the model into their apps, plus a quick checklist to verify that the deployment path matches the target environment. You want a repeatable, low-friction handoff that reduces the chance of "it runs on my

machine but not in production." Think of your package as a small bridge between model development and real-world use.

5) Test with end-to-end scenarios before going live. Run the model on the full inference pipeline you expect users to see: pre-processing, the model itself, post-processing, and any decision logic. Use realistic or synthetic data that mirrors production conditions. Check for memory usage, startup time, and how the system handles bursts of requests. If you can simulate user flows, you'll spot bottlenecks early and can fix them before customers experience delays or faults. Even when things go smoothly, keep a watchful eye on how the model's outputs are used downstream—sometimes small discrepancies

in preprocessing can cascade into noticeable differences in results.

Two micro-cases to illustrate the steps

- Case A: A lightweight image classifier for a mobile app. You export a compact TorchScript version of your model, apply post-training quantization to make it run efficiently on phones, and test CPU latency on a mid-range device. You verify that the accuracy remains within an acceptable range for everyday use, then package the runtime with a small setup script and a user-facing explanation of any minor accuracy trade-offs.

- Case B: A medium-size object detector deployed in a cloud service. You export to ONNX to facilitate running on a diverse set of back-ends, enable a TensorRT-accelerated path on Nvidia GPUs, and profile latency under concurrent loads. You find a sweet spot where throughput stays high and per-image latency remains below your target. You document the chosen path and note any minor changes in post-processing that came with the acceleration.

Edge vs cloud deployment considerations and hardware choices

1) Define the deployment target early. Edge deployment means running the model on devices near the user, like smartphones, cameras, or embedded gadgets. Cloud deployment means sending data to remote servers where you can leverage larger, more capable hardware. Your choice affects latency tolerance, privacy, bandwidth, and how you handle updates. If you need instant responses and privacy, edge makes a lot of sense. If your goal is to handle many users with heavy models, cloud deployment can scale more easily. Knowing the audience and constraints up front helps you pick the right path rather than trying to retrofit later.

2) Size and complexity matter for the chosen hardware. On the edge, you'll often favor smaller, faster models with local inference. On the cloud, you can afford larger models that produce higher accuracy or richer outputs. The hardware landscape looks different in each setting: edge devices may use CPUs, mobile GPUs, or dedicated neural accelerators; cloud environments commonly rely on multi-GPU servers, optimized inference engines, or specialized accelerators. The guiding idea is to match the model's footprint to the device's capabilities, so you don't overpromise speed or underdeliver accuracy.

3) Privacy, bandwidth, and offline operation shape decisions. Edge deployment minimizes data

leaving the device, which is good for privacy-sensitive applications and low-bandwidth contexts. Cloud deployment can collect aggregate signals, support more powerful models, and simplify updates. If your use case involves sensitive data or limited network access, design for edge-first operation with safe fallbacks to cloud only when necessary. If continual updates and heavy compute are more important, plan for a cloud-heavy workflow with secure data handling and clear data policies.

4) Plan for hardware heterogeneity. In edge environments, devices vary widely in CPU speed, memory, and available accelerators. Your deployment strategy should tolerate this variability.

In the cloud, you still face diversity across instance types and regions, but you can standardize the stack more easily. Build a flexible deployment recipe that can adapt to different runtimes and hardware accelerators without reworking the whole model. This reduces surprises when you reach new users or expand to new devices.

5) Testing and updating strategies matter more than you might think. Edge deployments typically require careful rollout plans because a faulty update can affect many users with limited ability to roll back quickly. Cloud deployments can push updates with canaries and quick rollback mechanisms, but you still need reliable versioning. The practical approach is to prepare multiple deployment paths,

test thoroughly in staging that mirrors production, and implement a simple rollback plan that you can execute in minutes if something goes wrong. You want to minimize downtime and maintain a straightforward path to fix issues.

Two micro-cases to illustrate edge vs cloud decisions

- Case C: A home security camera uses edge inference on-device to detect motion and potential intruders. The model is lightweight, runs on an integrated accelerator, and updates are delivered through a controlled app store channel. You monitor device performance and push small, incremental updates to improve accuracy without requiring users to reconfigure anything.

- Case D: A wildlife monitoring service processes thousands of images in the cloud to identify species and track populations. You deploy a larger, more accurate model on cloud GPUs and use a fast edge path for pre-filtering. Updates are rolled out gradually with canary checks, and you keep a robust model registry to track versions across regions.

Monitoring performance in production, versioning, and rollbacks

1) Build practical monitoring dashboards. Track latency, throughput, and error rates in production, plus occasional accuracy checks on a sample of outputs. Collect logs that help you trace decisions from raw image to final label. Your system should highlight outliers quickly, so you can investigate and fix any drift or unexpected behavior. The goal is to catch problems early, not after users notice them.

2) Version your models clearly. Use a simple, explicit versioning scheme and a central registry so teams know exactly which model is in use, where it came from, and what data it was trained on. Document key assumptions, such as input size, preprocessing steps, and supported hardware. When a newer version is better, you can route users

to the improved model step by step, rather than swapping everything at once. Clear versioning reduces confusion and speeds up debugging when issues arise.

3) Plan canary releases and rollbacks. A canary deployment introduces a new model to a small subset of traffic to observe how it behaves under real conditions before a full rollout. If metrics stay healthy, you expand gradually; if they deteriorate, you roll back quickly. Build in automated checks that trigger a rollback if latency, error rate, or a key accuracy metric crosses a threshold. A clear rollback protocol saves time and protects user experience.

4) Detect drift and data changes. Production images may drift from your training data in lighting, composition, or content. Having lightweight drift checks helps you decide when to re-train or fine-tune. Treat drift as a signal that your model needs attention, not as a failure to be masked. You don't need to chase every anomaly, but you should respond to patterns that meaningfully affect results.

5) Prepare for maintenance and updates. Your deployment plan should include routine updates, security patches, and routine health checks. Make updates predictable and reversible. Keep a short, accessible changelog for stakeholders so everyone understands what changed and why. The aim is

continuity of service with clear paths to improvements and fixes.

Two micro-cases to illustrate monitoring and versioning

- Case E: A photo-filter app uses edge inference, and you implement a canary rollout for a new color-detection model. You monitor latency and user-reported quality, and you can switch back to the previous version within minutes if a spike appears in error signals.

- Case F: A medical-imaging aid runs in the cloud with a strict versioning protocol. Each model version is registered, tested against a validation suite, and tagged with its training data snapshot. Updates are staged across regions, and rollback plans exist for any region that shows trouble.

Key Takeaway: Planning for deployment, hardware, and ongoing monitoring upfront saves time, reduces risk, and keeps your image-recognition project reliable as it scales.

Coming up next

Subtittle: Ethics, Robustness, and Future Directions

Addressing bias, privacy, and ethical data collection practices

Defenses against adversarial examples and robustness testing

Emerging trends: self-supervised learning, multimodal models, and continual learning

Chapter 10

Ethics, Robustness, and Future Directions

Outcome: You will learn practical, beginner-friendly ways to handle ethics in image recognition, strengthen robustness against tricky inputs, and spot near-future trends you can explore on your own.

Ethics, Bias, and Data Practices

You start with the idea that data shape models. If the data are biased or collected without care for privacy, the model may make unfair mistakes or hurt people. That's not acceptable, and it's easy to address if you build in simple, repeatable practices from the start.

1) Audit for representation and bias

Look at your data like a fairness thermos. If a lot of images come from one place or one group, you might miss others. Your step is to check who is in your data and who is not. The rationale is simple: the more diverse your examples, the less likely the model will overfit to one look or one scene. Act by listing key groups or categories you see and noting gaps. If gaps exist, plan small data additions that fill those gaps.

2) Document data provenance and consent

Know where each image comes from and what you're allowed to do with it. The practice is to keep a short record for each batch: who provided it, how it was collected, and what consent or rights you have to use it for training. The rationale is accountability. When questions arise about responsibility or rights, you can point to a clear trail.

3) Minimize collection and protect privacy

Ask yourself if you truly need every bit of data you collect. If you don't, leave it out. When you must include sensitive information, apply privacy protections such as de-identification and masking of personal details. The reason is simple: privacy protects people and also keeps you out of avoidable trouble. You can blur faces or remove metadata that isn't essential to the task.

4) Strengthen labeling quality and fairness reviews

Labels steer learning. If labeling is biased or inconsistent, the model learns bad patterns. Create simple checks: sample labels, recalc a portion with a second rater, and look for obvious disagreements. The rationale is to catch mistakes early. When disagreements arise, discuss and harmonize the labeling approach so it stays fair across categories.

5) Build governance and ongoing ethics reviews

Treat ethics like a living procedure, not a one-off checkbox. Schedule regular reviews with teammates who can spot problems you might miss. The rationale is to catch evolving risks as data, tasks, and social context shift. A practical approach is a quarterly ethics quick-check that asks: Are we still fair across groups? Is consent intact? Are privacy protections working?

6) Communicate limits and fairness to users

Be transparent about what your model can and cannot do, and what data it uses. A clear explanation builds trust and manages expectations. The rationale is that informed users can decide how they want to engage with your tool. A practical step is to publish a short user-facing note that describes data sources, privacy protections, and known limitations without exposing sensitive details.

Two micro-cases to ground these ideas

Example 1: A fashion-app dataset leans heavily toward images of light-skinned models. You notice accuracy dips on darker-skinned examples during testing. You respond by adding diverse images from new sources, retraining, and rechecking performance across skin tones. The result: fairness improves, and users feel more included.

Example 2: An image app analyzes street scenes and saves location tags. You decide to blur or remove exact GPS coordinates and redact faces in shared outputs. Users notice fewer privacy worries, and you notice fewer reports about misuse. This shift keeps your project safer and more trustworthy without sacrificing core functionality.

Templates and quick tools you can copy

Ethics Review Checklist

- Data provenance: source, consent, rights for training

- Representation: identify underrepresented groups and plan additions

- Privacy safeguards: anonymization, masking, minimum data use

- Labeling quality: inter-rater checks, disagreement resolution

- Transparency: who uses the model, what it can and cannot do

- Governance: scheduled ethics reviews, response plans for issues

- User communication: clear notes about data and limits

Robustness and Adversarial Defenses

You'll hear about "adversarial examples" as tiny tricks that trick a model into the wrong answer. They show you fragility in how the model processes information. The goal here is not to make the model perfect, but to make it reliable enough for real-world use, where data can be messy and attackers may test boundaries. You can improve resilience with simple, practical steps that fit into a beginner's workflow.

1) Define the threat model you care about

Ask: What kinds of tricky inputs do you expect in real use? Do you worry about small pixel tweaks, unusual lighting, or images from unfamiliar cameras? The rationale is to focus your efforts on the kinds of disturbances that matter most for your task. Write down a short list of perturbations you want to handle.

2) Use robust training and data augmentation

Train with a wider variety of inputs and deliberate small changes to pictures. The idea is to teach the model to see the real shape of objects even when color, brightness, or minor details shift. The rationale is simple: broadened experience reduces sensitivity to tiny tricks and helps generalization. A practical approach is to mix through-the-camera variations, color jitter, blurring, and noise during training.

3) Add input validation and anomaly detection

If something feels off at inference time, catch it before the model decides. Build a lightweight check for unusual patterns, like images that are far from anything the model has seen. The rationale is to stop obviously suspicious inputs from driving a wrong decision. If a check flags a suspect input, you can route it for human review or return a safe fallback.

4) Test robustness with perturbations and transformations

Create a small suite of tests that apply common changes to test images: brightness shifts, slight rotations, crops, and compression. The rationale is to measure how sensitive the model is to everyday variation. Track performance metrics under these tests to see where you need to harden the model.

5) Monitor deployment for drift and attack attempts

In production, data can drift away from what you trained on. Set up simple monitoring: watch for sudden drops in accuracy, unusual input types, or spikes in suspicious activity. The rationale is early warning. When you see drift, plan a data refresh or a targeted re-training cycle.

6) Plan for updates and re-training

Robustness is not a one-time fix. Schedule regular checks and updates so your model stays reliable as data changes. The rationale is long-term reliability. Keep a log of changes and run your test suite after every major update.

Two micro-cases to illustrate

Example 1: A small image classifier trained on everyday objects faces trouble when images are slightly darkened. You add brightness-controlled augmentations and a mild amount of noise during training. After re-training, accuracy under darker lighting improves, and the model feels steadier in dim conditions.

Example 2: A street-scene detector receives some unusual, heavily compressed images from a new camera. Anomaly checks flag these as outliers, and you route them to a human reviewer rather than risking a wrong label. Confidence in automated decisions rises, and you preserve safety.

Templates and quick tools you can copy

Robustness Testing Plan

- Threat model: list expected perturbations and scenarios

- Data augmentation strategy: describe the types and intensity

- Validation checks: criteria that indicate an input is suspicious

- Test suite: images or simulations for brightness, rotation, crop, and compression

- Monitoring plan: metrics to track, alert thresholds, and review cadence

- Update cycle: schedule for retraining and revalidation

Emerging Trends: Self-Supervised Learning, Multimodal Models, and Continual Learning

This is where you peek at what comes next and why it matters. These trends change how you learn from data, how you connect different kinds of information, and how a model can adapt over time without forgetting what it already knows.

Self-Supervised Learning

What it is: systems that learn useful representations from unlabeled data by solving tasks that don't require humans to annotate everything. The benefit is you can leverage huge pools of images to teach the model to understand shapes, textures, and relations, then fine-tune with a smaller set of labeled data. The caveat: it often needs more compute and careful design to ensure the learned features align with your real task.

Two practical implications: you can build stronger feature extractors with less labeled data, and you can broaden the kinds of images your model understands by tapping into vast, unlabeled collections. Realistic micro-case: you take a large unlabeled image set, train a self-supervised encoder, and then fine-tune a small labeled set for a niche classification task. You might find better generalization with fewer labels, especially in niche domains.

Multimodal Models

What it is: models that learn from more than one kind of information, such as images plus text, or images plus audio. The advantage is richer representations and often better accuracy because additional context helps disambiguate visual cues. The caveat: data alignment and bias become more complex. You need paired data (for example, an image with a caption) and careful handling of mismatches.

Two practical implications: you can improve recognition by using captions or descriptions to anchor what's in an image, and you can build more versatile tools that respond to natural language prompts. Micro-case: your image classifier also considers a caption during decision-making, helping distinguish similar-looking objects when text hints are available. You can often achieve better performance with only modest improvements in data collection if you pair the right modalities.

Continual Learning

What it is: systems that learn new tasks or adapt to new data over time without forgetting what they already learned. The benefit is models that stay relevant as scenes, products, or environments change. The caveat: models can “forget” earlier knowledge if updates aren’t carefully managed, a problem called catastrophic forgetting.

Two practical implications: you can keep your model fresh by adding new data in small steps, and you can design safeguards to keep older skills alive while adding new ones. Micro-case: you deploy a new class and show how the model gradually learns to recognize it while preserving accuracy on older classes through periodic rehearsals or regularization techniques.

Templates and practical tools for trends

Self-Supervised Experiment Plan

- Task choice: pick a self-supervised objective that matches your data (e.g., predicting image parts or transformations)

Data selection: assemble a large unlabeled image collection

- Fine-tuning strategy: specify how much labeled data you will use for the downstream task

- Evaluation: decide metrics and a simple baseline to compare against

Multimodal Data Alignment Checklist

- Data pairs: ensure each image has a compatible text or audio description

- Alignment validation: check how often descriptions match the visual content

- Bias check: look for skew in descriptions that could bias the model

- Safety guardrails: define limits for relying on non-visual information

Continual Learning Plan Template

- Task log: list tasks or data streams to learn incrementally

- Memory strategy: choose rehearsal, regularization, or architecture changes

- Evaluation schedule: set tests to verify no forgetting on old tasks

- Update cadence: plan when to retrain or adjust the system

Exercises (2–4)

1) Ethics quick-check (15 minutes). Review your current data sources and answer: Are there obvious biases or privacy concerns? Document two concrete

improvements you could make today. Measure progress by updating your data-provenance notes and listing at least two bias-risk notes you identified.

2) Robustness mini-test (20 minutes). Pick one common perturbation (brightness change, a slight crop, or compression). Apply it to a small batch of test images and record whether the model's labels stay the same. If accuracy drops, outline two simple augmentation or training changes you could try in a single afternoon.

3) Trend exploration sprint (25 minutes). Choose one emerging trend (self-supervised learning,

multimodal models, or continual learning). Describe in two short paragraphs how it could help your current project, plus one practical experiment you could run with modest resources to test the idea.

Troubleshooting

- Problem: Privacy concerns keep coming up in reviews.

Quick fix: Document clearly what data is collected, how it's used, and what protections exist; bring in a privacy-by-design checklist and adjust data collection accordingly.

- Problem: Your robustness tests show surprising failures on one type of input.

Quick fix: Add targeted augmentations for that input type during training, and consider a small pilot test with real-world samples from the field.

- Problem: You're unsure how to balance self-supervised learning with labeled data.

Quick fix: Start with a simple hybrid approach—learn using self-supervised methods on unlabeled data to build features, then fine-tune with your labeled set. Compare results to a purely supervised baseline.

- Problem: Multimodal data introduces alignment issues.

Quick fix: Begin with a modest paired dataset (images plus captions), verify alignment quality, and control for bias by auditing caption sources for biased language or misrepresentation.

Tools, templates, and quick-start templates

Ethics and Privacy Template

- Data sources and consent status

- Representation gaps and mitigation plan

- Labeling fairness checks and review cadence

- Privacy protections implemented (anonymization, masking)
- Transparency notes for users
- Governance schedule and escalation path

Robustness Plan Template

- Threat model summary
- Data augmentation and training changes
- Validation checks and anomaly detection
- Test suite with perturbations
- Production monitoring setup
- Update and retraining plan

Future Trends Experiment Template

- Trend choice and rationale

- Data and compute requirements

- Pilot objective and success metrics

- Evaluation plan and decision criteria

- Documented learnings and next steps

Ending and transition

As you close this chapter, you've built a toolkit that helps you work responsibly today while staying curious about what comes next. The next chapter will walk you through turning these ideas into practical image-recognition systems you can train, evaluate, and deploy, with a focus on turning theory into reliable, real-world performance.

Key Takeaway: Ethical awareness, robustness planning, and curiosity about new trends together keep image-recognition work responsible, reliable, and ready to evolve. Transition: In the next chapter, you'll apply these principles to building and testing actual image-recognition models, step by step, so you can see how ethics, resilience, and future directions translate into a working system.

Dear Reader,

Thank you for exploring this series focused on failures and the power of comeback stories. If you find value in these stories and believe in the importance of embracing setbacks as part of growth, we appreciate your support. Please consider sharing a positive review on the platform where you accessed this series.

Your feedback helps spread the message, inspiring more young readers to see challenges as opportunities and to believe in their potential. We understand that mistakes happen, and we thank you for your understanding.

www.ingramcontent.com/pod-product-compliance
Lightning Source LLC
LaVergne TN
LVHW022210200926
848481LV00006B/1913
9798295535468